Relevant Programs that bring RESULTS!

www.MakeAWayNow.com

10 THINGS EVERY LEADER MUST KNOW

The Rules to the Game Called Life

By Hotep

10 Things Every Leader Must Know

www.hustleuniversity.org

ISBN #978-0-9825976-3-7

Published by: Hustle U Inc.

Hustle University its logos and marks are trademarks of Hustle U Inc.

Manufactured in the United States of America

Printed by Selfpublishing.com

First Printing, October 2010

Photography by OPP Studios

PUBLISHER'S NOTE: This work is a labor of love. It is the result of my attending the **School of Hard Knocks** where I received a B.A. in *Failed Ideas*, a Masters Degree in *Bad Investments*, and a PhD in *Poor Time Management*. Names, characters, places, and incidents are either the product of the author's experiences or are used with permission, and any resemblance to actual persons, living or dead, business establishments, events, or locales is entirely on purpose.

To my parents, Felicia A. Scotland AND Ramon A. Benzo (RIP), Thank you for naming me after great people and making sure I grow into the crown that you placed soaring above my head. It is only by standing on your shoulders that I am able to reach so high!

To my Wife, You are the apple of my eye; the Sun in my sky. Everybody knows I love my Babykakes!

To my heroes, Marcus Garvey, Malcolm X, and Muhammad Ali.

I also dedicate this book to everyone whose life has inspired me, and to everyone that this book will touch. Manifest your Destiny!

Aight!

Peace!

ACKNOWLEDGEMENTS:

Mom- who continues to encourage me to do more, become better and greater, **Pops**- for providing me with the studies of ancient African Culture and Eastern theology and philosophy, **My Wife** for keeping me balanced and grounded, **Grandma Kenni & Grandma Benzo**- for being the roots of our family trees. **Dr. Coleman** for spiritual guidance, **Big Tah** (my brother from another mother) for dropping the seed of the idea for me to write an actual book, **Fort Knox** for being a "nice guy" (you're still the livest brother I know), **Nancy Gilliam** and **Denise Spiller** of AALM for holding the best conference I'd ever attended (it is because of your event that I decided to write this book!), **Wess** (fellow Garveyite)- you are the TRUE documentarian! Thank you for rollin' with me. **Leslie Greene**- for believing in my documentary's vision b4 it was manifested, **Kim Wilson**- for jump-starting my filmmaking career. **Troya Sampson** for being the first person to REALLY get behind my vision and *cheerlead* for Hotep & Skinnymen Productions (you're forever my ace!), **Leticia** (Docugraphix)- for being my first major sponsor. **Mimi Cartier** – for continually being such a blessing and so thoughtful, **Kehinde Thompson**- the hottest photographer I know (it's your turn)! **KeyC**- for years of tech support and reliability. **Nadra**- one of the few truly GOOD BROTHERS I know, **Caustic Mimi**- ("*Goin' to the Grammys*") you're my sister-in-arms and I got your back! **Rosalind**- the epitome of Hottentot Venus- you were MY counselor! **Bro Malik**- the other good brother I know. To all the contributing writers- your life lessons are priceless! Thank you for sharing them. To those I missed.....my humble apologies. I love you all!

TABLE OF CONTENTS

FOREWORD:

My personal story is one of an individual who could never find a way; ......so he MADE a way.

My journey as an entrepreneur started in 1991 when my brothers and I decided we wanted to become famous Hip-Hop artists. Our efforts led us to a meeting with executives at Sony Records in 1992. It was at this meeting that I first realized my own propensity for leadership.

After hearing our demo, the executives expressed interest; but requested that we make certain changes to our appearance and music in order to get their full approval. My brothers and I didn't agree with Sony's recommendations. While we could have followed their directions (like many artists do), I convinced my brothers to walk the road less traveled. We decided to release our music on our own; without the big marketing budget and distribution power that a major label like Sony had.

Our success as independent musicians was meager. We had only a small following of fans in the local Atlanta Hip-Hop community; and I can't remember making much money at all. **But what I do recall is the huge boost of confidence I received from the experience.**

Once I learned that I could create and sell professional quality products that were comparable to what major corporations produced, I was forever empowered with the belief that **there was nothing I couldn't accomplish**.

This belief was the single most important factor in my entrepreneurial journey.

Over the years, I endeavored to start other ventures. For each, I initially sought help from others; but after being turned down numerous times, I found myself having to launch those businesses on my own. I was only able to do this because **I believed it was possible**.

While most of my peers left their destiny in the hands of others by **waiting** for opportunities, I was manifesting my own destiny by **creating** opportunities.

I developed a reputation for being a person that was able to *make it happen*. After years of blazing trails in the independent music, film and publishing industries, I looked behind me and saw an army of people following the example I was setting. What I realized is that while people liked what I was doing, they were most interested in learning HOW I DID IT.

In the year 2005, I assembled a collection of power principles that was to later become my single most popular creation. I called this collection, **The Hustler's 10 Commandments**. I first premiered The Hustler's 10 in my documentary entitled, *The Hustler's Guide To The Entertainment Industry*. The film was an attempt to provide entrepreneurs with the strategies that I learned and was using to create a consistent habit of success.

As I toured with the film, I noticed that most of the questions I was being asked were centered on The Hustler's 10 Commandments. This further cemented in my mind the idea that people liked what I did, but they were most interested in learning HOW I DID IT.

I never considered writing a book as an option. Ironically, in the documentary, I actually mentioned that I would, *"never write a book because (black people) don't read."* To be honest, the only reason why I wrote the book, *The Hustler's 10 Commandments* was to protect myself from someone stealing my intellectual property. I DID NOT THINK PEOPLE WOULD ACTUALLY BUY THE BOOK.

After selling tens of thousands of copies (primarily to those same black people I previously thought didn't read), I realized I was on to something huge! Through The Hustler's 10 Commandments, I have been able to reach a large audience of people that have been traditionally underserved and overlooked by self-help gurus and empowerment leaders in the past. I found myself in a unique position which allowed me to connect entrepreneurs from, *"the streets to the executive suites"*. It was with this realization that I finally accepted my position of leadership.

I built **Hustle University** as a way to pull seekers of empowerment together and formally teach the strategies contained in The Hustler's 10 Commandments to a broader audience. I also decided to enter the education market because I found that I was able to use the same 10 principles to motivate youth as well.

The Hustler's 10 Commandments was a hit; and since I was a Morehouse College graduate, a schoolteacher, and because a good number of my followers were young black males, I just knew I could easily get schools and youth organizations to purchase The Hustler's 10 Commandments for their students.

Boy, was I WRONG!

It turned out that regardless of the proven effectiveness of my work; and although I made all attempts to provide proper context and definitions, the words

Hustle and *Hustler* came with too much negative baggage for federally funded institutions to handle.

After a few years of trying to sift through all the bureaucratic red tape, I decided to try an approach more familiar to me.
Since I couldn't *find a way* to get The Hustler's 10 Commandments into school systems and youth organizations on a large scale…. I made a way!

Welcome to **10 Things Every Leader MUST Know!**

They say, *"Don't judge a book by its cover,"* but everybody does.

INTRODUCTION:

The subtitle to 10 Things Every Leader MUST Know is, **The Rules to the Game Called Life**. I named it this because I've learned at an early age that life truly is a game. It's a very serious game in which we each only have one man left to *"play"* with. Life has rules to play by, and regulations that govern it. And just like every game, life can be fun to play for some; but for others, it can be a miserable experience. This is usually dependent on whether or not a person is winning or losing.

The Winner:

When a person knows how to play a game, they become good at it. They win. The game is fun. The person feels confident. This person wants to play often and seeks even more challenges because they want to win again and again. They make winning look easy. Other people want to be on their team. A winner enjoys the game because they know they can control the outcome. Therefore, they can create whatever type of experience they choose.

The Loser:

When a person does not know how to play a game, they often lose. Losers don't like the game. They think the game is difficult. This person would rather not play the game so they can avoid more losses. They often complain about the game being unfair and blame winners for "cheating". Nobody wants to play with a loser. Losers do not enjoy the game because their past losses have made them feel unsure of themselves. They cannot control the outcome of their experience and believe that chances are, whatever the outcome, it will surely be another loss.

Doesn't that sound familiar?

The major difference between winners and losers is their ability to control the outcome of the game. But the fact of the matter is... WE ALL CONTROL THE OUTCOMES OF OUR GAMES.

Once a person knows and applies the rules of the game, they can maneuver more effectively through it. When a person accepts the rules, they can better predict the outcomes of their decisions. If a person decides to ignore the rules, the game will become more difficult to play; yet, it is still their choice to do so.

If a person is alive, the game is on. It never pauses or stops. Therefore, if a person doesn't take control of their game (by refusing to play or not knowing how to play) theirs will be controlled by others. This is why some people cannot control the outcome of their lives and end up losing. They've let go of the steering wheel and allowed other people to direct their path. When a person does this, they will be used and victimized repeatedly. Their life will be.... out of control.

The good news is that any person can take back the controls of their game whenever they decide to. AND (if they know and apply the rules), they can LEAD their life and create any type of wonderful experience they choose.

Yes! We are all leaders.

The question is: **In what direction are you leading YOUR life?**

"Lead your life, or you will always be mis-led by others." - Hotep

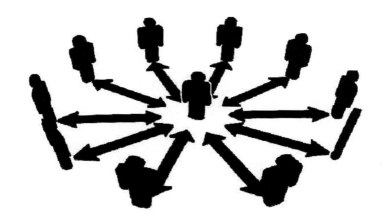

THE 1ST THING
EVERY LEADER
MUST KNOW

YOUR NETWORK IS YOUR NET WORTH.

CHAPTER 1: YOUR NETWORK IS YOUR NET WORTH

Net worth is commonly known as the difference between what you *own* and what you *owe*. You can figure your net worth by adding all your debts (credit cards, mortgages, car loans, and/or anything else you owe) and subtracting that sum from your total assets (home value, stocks, cash, furniture, electronics and anything else you own of value).

Net worth is not an actual pile of physical dollars, but more a summation of the *potential dollar amount* that your assets would bear if you liquidated (sold) them. It is with this same summation of **potential** that we can include our network (friends, crew, gang, homies, posse) as assets too.

"Birds of a feather, flock together."

Remember when you were little, and your mother told you to be careful who you choose as friends? Well, that advice doesn't change with age. Your friends will either help bring you up, or take you down. They can be **assets** or **liabilities**.

It was once suggested to me that I make a list of people in my life that I can count **on**, and those I can count **out**. Doing so, (and spending the majority of my time with those that I could count on) drastically improved my business and social life. The same can and will happen for you.

"If you hang around 4 broke people, you're bound to be the 5th".

This saying would still hold true if you replaced the word *broke* with *rich*, *positive*, *smart* or any other adjective you choose. Such is the power of your **network**.

My cousin calls his network his "Circle of Influence". I think this is a very appropriate term because it recognizes the amazing influence those we surround ourselves with have on us. Your business will flourish if you hang around business savvy people. Your life will start to seem so much more beautiful if your friends are positive and optimistic. You will never be homeless, without food, clothes or money if your circle is affluent. That's because your Network is your Net Worth!

LIFE LESSON:

I have always been one who believed in networking, but it wasn't until very recently that I discovered the truth behind the idea; your network is your net worth.

After having been away from the literary and media industries for a little over fifteen years, I slowly began transitioning myself back into the business. I started seeking opportunities to promote my children's book which I had self-published. With the aid of the Internet, I began tapping into sources and building a network that would assist me in fulfilling my quest.

I discovered there were many people out there who had an interest in what I was doing and sincerely wanted to help. I received invitations to different events and accepted most. During my travels, I continued to meet like-minded individuals, and my network continued to grow.

As a firm believer in the power of giving, I made it my business to do whatever I could to help someone achieve his or her goals and visions. This included not only disseminating information, but also seizing opportunities to make connections between people that could benefit from each other's talents and experiences. The more that I helped others, the more "fuel" I received to keep the fire of my vision and purpose burning.

The recognition of the value, or net worth of my network came during the African American Literary and Media Conference, which was held February 2006 in Reno, Nevada. This was the AALAM Group's first conference, and it was our vision to create an atmosphere where novices and professionals would be able to receive the tools and inspiration needed to navigate their way through the literary and media industries. My partner Denise and I were faced with many challenges and seemingly insurmountable obstacles. There were critical moments where giving up was the option of choice, but we decided to make the sacrifice and do whatever it would take to make the conference happen.

It was a decision that transformed our lives forever. During that weekend, our network was drawn together from all points within the United States. There are no words to describe the power and synergy that was experienced. People's lives were changed. Relationships were solidified. Projects were birthed. Strength to continue was found in our network.

That weekend helped me discover the importance of being surrounded by positive like-minded individuals who understand the power of giving as well as receiving. No one person can achieve

greatness and realize the power of possibility remaining inside of self. Yes, it is true that your sense of self worth is important, but ultimately it is your network that is your net worth!
- Nancy Gilliam

TASKS:

1) Make a list of the people you can *COUNT ON* and those you can *COUNT OUT*.
2) Build your own" circle of influence" from the people you can *count on.*
3) Spend less time with the people you can *count out.*
4) Identify someone that is successful in your field. See if you can intern for them or have them mentor you.
5) Attend conferences, networking socials and online groups where people of similar interest or goals are.

It was at AALAM that Hotep got the idea to write The Hustler's 10 Commandments book. He also met Essence best-selling author **Omar Tyree** (above) and **Tyson Hall** (right); who both became part of Hotep's network and consequently, contributing authors to this book.

THE 2ND THING
EVERY LEADER
MUST KNOW

IMAGE IS EVERYTHING.

CHAPTER 2: IMAGE IS EVERYTHING

They say we should never judge a book by its cover, but it's the *cover* that makes us want to open the book in the first place.

What is truth? Truth is NOT a matter of fact. History has shown us all, that *truth* is only an **idea** that is commonly accepted. Yet laws, policy and judgments are often erroneously made based off of these ideas everyday.

At one time, each of these ideas was once "true":

1) The Earth is flat.
2) Christopher Columbus discovered America.
3) Africa has made no significant contribution to the world.
4) Cocaine is good for you and should be used daily.

Get the picture? Truth is only what we **perceive** it to be; this is why *image* is key.

Whether right or wrong, the true power of image is the fact that people make **DECISIONS** based on their perception of things. Consumers buy products because of their *perception* of it. People chose mates because of their *perception* of the other person. Citizens choose leaders based on their *perception* of that candidate. Policemen and judges make decisions about a person's guilt (and ultimately their freedom) according to their *perception* of the individual. Where is truth in any of these examples? The fact of the matter is: **very little of what we do is based on actual truth.**

God is the only truth. As mere mortals, we can only hope that our perception of things is actually *true*. In the meantime, we must respect the great power of perception and decide how we can use imagery to our benefit. If you know that people are making life-changing **DECISIONS** about you (and your business) based on image, what can be done to make sure that their perception of you is positive?

Apply the power of perception to your daily practices and you can transform your identity and success ratio immediately. Image is EVERYTHING.

LIFE LESSON:

Image is everything! For a decade now I have been a natural wearing, strong looking, and unapproachable black woman. My natural made me look like a piece of brick. That was good for me in my personal life, meaning, I had control over things. If I didn't want to be bothered by certain folks, my demeanor would let them know. This was also a bad thing because whether I knew it or not, I seemed to look limited to revolutionary type roles, events, and things. How was I to get the world to realize I was far more than the length of my afro? How was I to let the business/entertainment world know, I wasn't going to commit arson on their property? Or that I wouldn't go on national television and advocate "killing whitey"?

In winter 2005, I actually decided to run an experiment. Now, I have a short processed look and my hair is similar to Nia Long's in "The Best Man". I slightly changed my attire to "simply sophisticated" and I wear eye make-up. I took my new look amongst my co-workers in the entertainment field and they lost their minds. People are digging this new look. Wow! I hadn't changed on the inside at all. I am still stern, intelligent, and no non-sense, but it seemed to not be a factor being I didn't look like Teflon in a dress. I am getting more compliments and people aren't intimidated by me.

Overall, the change was healthy and is deeming itself profitable. Since image is everything, I'm not saying "fake it, til you make it"; I'm saying, "If it ain't working, CHANGE IT!

- Queen (Shanikra Hankins)

TASKS:

1) Make sure your website or product exterior look exceptionally good.
2) Dress the part. *The way you DRESS determines the way you will be ADDRESSED.*
3) Speak clearly and with confidence.
4) Create promotional material to support your business (biz cards, flyers, t-shirts)
5) Keep your vehicle looking nice and well maintained. Of course, a luxury vehicle will make you appear to have money. But please don't over extend your finances for a car.
6) *Peep Game!* Pay attention to Flyers, CDs, Books or DVD covers that catch your eye. Take the time to identify WHY you noticed them and implement those aspects into your own designs.

"With the right mentality, nothing can **STOP** you. With the wrong mentality, nothing can **SAVE** you!" -Hotep

Practicing what he preaches, Hotep has an ensemble of high-impact marketing materials (like his infamous bookmarks) that continue to outshine the competition and inspire business owners.

* Note that he is wearing a suit in this image, which creates a perception of intelligence, wealth and affluence.

THE 3RD THING EVERY LEADER MUST KNOW

THE EARLY BIRD GETS THE WORM.

CHAPTER 3: THE EARLY BIRD GETS THE WORM

This chapter is personally relevant to me. I have always struggled with being on time. I've been late for everything from dates, to events, to meetings and airplane flights. A friend once joked and said that I will be late to my own funeral. So, dear readers, please know that I write these words for my own benefit as much as I do for yours.

The concept of time must be respected and held almost sacredly. Why? Because **time is one of the very few things in life that never repeats itself.** Once it's gone, it's gone...forever! So, until someone invents a way for humans to travel back in time... Respect it!

In order to maximize the opportunities that are opened before us, we must arrive **on time** to receive them. No. Scratch that.... not "*on time*".........we need to be EARLY!

A school principal once told me, *"To be on time, is to be late"*. The truth in this statement wasn't actually apparent to me until I began writing this book.

Please follow this scenario:

You are right on time for your meeting with a record label CEO, book publisher, film distributor....whatever. You walk into her office, make your presentation, ask your questions, smile, shake hands and leave the meeting feeling confident that it went well.....and it did!

*However, because you were simply **on time**, you missed the opportunity to check your appearance in the restroom. If you had, you would have noticed that your zipper was open. Because you were simply **on*** *time*, *you also missed hearing the CEO comment on a meeting she had last week. If you had been there to hear her comments, you would have known not to give her so many compliments (she really hates that). You also missed her secretary's phone conversation. If you were early enough to hear it, you would have known that a new position at the office had opened up. A position you would have loved to apply for.*

Unfortunately for you, the guy that had a meeting with the CEO after yours was an hour EARLY. He heard all of the conversations and was able to check his appearance. He was relaxed, ready to inquire about the job opening and would not comment on the CEO's good looks.

Who do YOU think made the most of their opportunity?

The EARLY BIRD got the worm!

LIFE LESSON:

I remember my freshman year of college at the University of Pittsburgh in August 1987. It was registration day and I was headed to one of the campus buildings to register for my classes that semester. I wasn't early that morning, and there was a long line in front of me to enter the building. But I noticed immediately that everyone was waiting to go inside one door when there four other doors available to enter the building. So I walked up past everyone in line and tried one of the other doors, and it opened. I walked right in past the line; and guess what happened after that.......... half of the other line followed me into the door.

So, although I was not early that day, I had the courage to be first, and being first is parallel to being early. They are similar in that you have no company there with you, and so you may feel awkward, inexperienced and afraid of what may happen. It takes courage and confidence to be first, and eagerness and promptness to be early. Well, generally, I'm an early riser, early starter, early arriver as well, which all lends itself to me being one who is brave, bold, and ready enough to start things on my own. In fact, my whole life has been that way. I was always starting things and getting there early to be first.

Anyway, that's exactly what I did in my career as a young writer. In 1991, among Terry McMillan, Bebe Moore Campbell, Walter Mosley, and E. Lynn Harris, I became the first and youngest author to write about contemporary urban streets since Donald Goines and Iceberg Slim. So I was early, I was first, I'll continue to reinvent the game and I'm still eating those juicy worms with more on the way (smile.)
- Omar Tyree

TASKS:

1) **Don't put off for tomorrow what you can do today.**
2) **Set your clock 30 minutes ahead of the actual time.**
3) **Act on your ideas before someone else does.**
4) **Arrive at meetings at least 20 minutes early.**
5) **Arrive at events an 30 minutes early.**
6) **Call to confirm appointments 1 hour prior to meeting time.**

7) Turn in assignments before their deadline.
8) Buy the web domain for your idea immediately.

THE 4TH THING EVERY LEADER MUST KNOW

IT'S LONELY AT THE TOP.

CHAPTER 4: IT'S LONELY AT THE TOP

While using the bathroom at a sports bar, I came across a posted article about Allen Iverson. It was in this unlikely place and from this *bad boy* athlete that I learned a great lesson. In the article was a quote from Iverson that went something like....

*"There are a million people that love me, and a **Billion** people that hate me. I think about those that love me, and keep it moving."*

This statement is the perfect acceptance speech for one that understands the next commandment.

It's lonely at the top.

If you look around yourself and notice you have a lot fewer peers than you used to, it may be a sign that you're getting closer to being successful in your field. Don't let your raggedy, good-for-nothing friends make you feel bad because you don't call and hang around them any more. That's the old crabs in a barrel routine; **they would rather pull you down, than see you get out!**

Understand this:

The masses of our world's population are **followers**, not *leaders*; **consumers**, not *producers*; **victims**, not *victors*. They watch too much TV, listen to too much radio and believe everything they see and hear. This phenomenon is no accident. In a capitalist democracy it is an absolute necessity!

Think about your Junior High School years:

As youth, we had the tendency to follow the crowd. We often suffered from the effects of peer pressure. Most of us sought to "*fit in*". For the intelligent, well-behaved child, this often meant **acting** ignorant; and doing things that led to trouble, bad health and lower achievement.

Well, the real world of adults isn't much different. But now, the "crowd" that many of us once sought to emulate is broke, troubled by legal issues, riddled with diseases and see little hope for a better future. **Who wants to be a part of that crowd?**

As you become increasingly successful, wealthy and wise; you will find that you have to distance yourself from your homies of the past. Don't let them run that *"You forgot where you came from"* speech.

You remember where you come from, but you **also know where you are going**. So get ready, cuz it's lonely at the top!

LIFE LESSON:

There is a price to pay for being successful, and most people don't want to pay it. That's why there's Lotto and a whole bunch of infomercials on TV late at night that sell you unrealistic ways to achieve "easy" success.

I manage several musical artists. Every time we reach a certain level of success (such as putting an album out, booking a major show or filming a DVD) other artists approach us begging to be managed by our management team. They see the effects, and want them too. So I direct them right to the cause that made the effect happen.

I invite them to join the team, but on a lower level than they expect. For example: I tell them that we only have room for a hype man when I know they want to be the main rapper. Or I tell them that we need a road manager when I know they would like to be a main manager. Am I just being mean and vindictive? No, I'm requesting that they go through the same process that everyone on the team went through to get where we're at. How does one know that they can handle the pressures of being on the top unless they've been through trials and tribulations?

When you climb to the top, you're forming muscles, courage and wherewithal that will aid you in staying at the top. That's why it's so lonely up there; because most people aren't strong enough to climb the mountain of success. It IS lonely at the top, and I'd rather be alone with my hard working self, than with a group of lazy tag-a-longs. The top of the pyramid is pointed for a reason.
- Big Tah

LIFE LESSON:

*Often times, you hear people say that it is lonely at the top, but what you don't hear people elaborate on is that it is just as lonely **getting** to the top. I am not at the peak of my career yet; however, I still experience loneliness in my quest to reach this point. As an Entertainment Attorney, I have encountered everything from men who reject me due to my earning potential to people being intimidated by my career to people asking me to compromise myself in order to get ahead. I have heard successful women speak of this before, but there is nothing like experiencing it* *for yourself. Despite these obstacles and barriers, I continue on the journey even when it means doing so alone.*

I have had to leave certain things and people behind in order to accomplish my goals. This has often left me alone to conquer unfamiliar territory, but that is a sacrifice that I willingly make to maximize my potential. Even some of my loved ones do not fully understand the path that I am on. At the end of day, I realize that trailblazers venture into unfamiliar places to make their mark even when it requires the dreadful loneliness that most people fear. It is lonely at the top; and also during the journey to the top as well, but sometimes it is the journey that makes the destination worth it all!
- Keisha R. Perry, Esq.

TASKS:

1) **Make your haters, your MOTIVATORS!**
2) **Seek QUALITY in relationships, not quantity.**
3) **Find peace and happiness in solitude.**
4) **Find a support group of like-minded individuals.**
5) **In times of loneliness, seek companionship in your work.**
6) **Love yourself enough to be happy BY yourself.**

THE 5TH THING EVERY LEADER MUST KNOW

SUCCESS- WHERE OPPORTUNITY MEETS PREPARATION.

CHAPTER 5: SUCCESS- WHERE OPPORTUNITY MEETS PREPARATION

"Tomorrow belongs to the people who prepare for it today". – **Malcolm X**

Everybody wants to be successful. The question is: *Are you ready for opportunity when it finally knocks*? Will you answer the door with your briefcase, laptop, cell phone and palm pilot ready to roll? Or will you be caught in your pajamas, yawning with cold in your eyes?

"To be prepared is EVERYTHING." (as told to me by my father).

Let's look at the entertainment/ media industries. Many people in these industries are in pursuit of receiving that ever elusive, life changing "deal". (Record deal, label deal, distribution deal, publishing deal, modeling deal...etc.) Most artists spend countless hours perfecting their craft, but **few** take the necessary steps to fully prepare themselves for the very opportunity that they seek. They may be talented, but most people in the entertainment/ media industries are undoubtedly NOT READY FOR THE BUSINESS OF "THE DEAL".

Don't put the horse before the carriage.

Whatever the goal, there are always requirements that must be met first. People have a tendency of focusing on the goal, without meeting the necessary requirements. Before a "deal" can be struck, there are many things that have to be in order. The more things a person has in order, the sooner a deal can occur. Without these things, there will be NO favorable deal.

Here are a few things that businesses (even artists) need in order to execute a speedy and fair deal: *copyright, trademark, business account, legal counsel, releases, clearances, resume, presskit, professional photo, bio, work samples, **reliable** computer/ internet access, phone and transportation.*

Are you <u>ready</u> for success?

All too often, the opportunity passes people by, OR they get offered a "deal" that is certainly not in their favor. Either way, **many fail to be successful, because they are simply not prepared.**

LIFE LESSON:

Recently I have been associated with several California companies that strive to create Urban based distribution deals for audio & video projects. With this in mind I have been soliciting projects from independent companies and producers for direct to DVD distribution. I came upon a project that had ALL of the features needed to become a major seller. BIG name Hip Hop artists, good filming techniques, strong soundtrack and a built in consumer following for sales.

I approached the company, had them send me a screener and forwarded their information to my clients in California. I also asked the company if they had ALL of the paperwork together to make this deal happen. Clearances on the individuals shot on camera, clearances on the music and ownership (copyright) of the material. Of course the company told me that they had everything I needed especially since I had the money to make this deal happen.

This company was offered a six-figure advance, a mid six-figure marketing budget and a guarantee for assistance in foreign markets. The contracts were sent and I started waiting for the company to send the required clearances so the check could be cut.

The company did not send in the materials or the contract for over 4 months. Upon further inquiry I finally found out that the person who shot the film never got anyone to sign off on the clearances, had never sent in a copyright form on the movie and had not published or cleared any of the music. ALL OF THIS AFTER THE DEAL HAD BEEN CUT.

Needless to say this project has died a slow death for it can never go to a mass audience. My relationship with the company has deteriorated based on the initial lies that they told and the distributor does not want to work with this company again.

Without the basic preparation this company missed their 15 minutes of fame and thousands of dollars in royalties.
- Allen Johnston

"People don't plan to fail, they FAIL TO PLAN!"

TASKS:

1) **ALWAYS carry a pen.**
2) **Carry a pen and paper to ALL meetings, workshops and conferences.**
3) **Keep business cards and press kits handy.**
4) **Create a folder on your desktop, laptop, smartphone for all your important**

promotional/ marketing materials. (including bio, discography, history, pictures, ads, reviews, letters.....etc).

5) Make sure all legal requirements are met. (copyright, trademark, contracts, releases, permissions.....etc).

Hotep was successful at getting his books into a major chain of bookstores (without the help of a major publisher or distributor) only because he was **prepared** with the necessary requirements. Look at the books they felt were comparable!

THE 6TH THING EVERY LEADER MUST KNOW

BUSINESS IS PERSONAL.

CHAPTER 6: BUSINESS IS PERSONAL

Don't ever let anyone sell you on the idea that a particular agreement, negotiation or transaction is, "*Business, not personal.*" That's a flat out lie! ALL BUSINESS is conducted off of the springboard of personal relationships.

Imagine this scenario:

It's a Friday night, and you decide to go out to the popular local nightclub owned by your good friend of 10 years. It is an especially chilly night. When you get there, you see your buddy at the entrance of the club. You also notice the line to get in is wrapped around the corner, and the VIP line isn't a much better option. Your friend, the club owner, sees you and motions for you to come to the entrance door. **What is your expectation at this moment?**

Undoubtedly, you are expecting some type of favor from your friend. Maybe he'll let you cut the line. Maybe he'll let you enter without being frisked. Maybe he'll let you in for free. Whatever it is, your expectation of special treatment was formed because of your relationship with the club owner. Don't worry, your expectation of favor/ special treatment and the granting thereof is normal everyday practice. It occurs at all levels of every industry; from the *streets*, to the *executive suites* and even as high as The White House!

Anyone who watched Michael Moore's documentary ***Fahrenheit 911*** saw how President George W. Bush basically hooked up all his buddies with great jobs in government and international business. It was obvious that many of the people he chose were not the best ones for the positions, but they all benefited from the same *"hook-up"* system outlined in the nightclub scenario.

Business IS Personal!

People hire employees that they *like*. People do business with businesses that they *like*. The best salespeople in the world all know the secret to high-powered selling is not in selling the product, but in selling THEMSELVES!

Even a person that has to fire or end a partnership with someone they like or are related to does so for personal reasons. Often times, we have to get rid of, or disassociate ourselves from people because they are costing us money or piece of mind. **What is more personal than that?**

No matter how you try to slice it, you can't deny the facts. As long as business continues to be conducted by *persons*, business will forever be **personal**!

LIFE LESSON:

People will give business and lend support to individuals that they like...PERIOD! That's business, and it's personal. As an actress I've had auditions, callbacks, and landed roles because the casting director or production assistant liked me and thought I was "sweet" and "kind". My instinctual response is, "well isn't everyone who is trying to get cast on a movie or television show, sweet, kind, patient, humble, etc". Their answers to me time, and time again are, "No!" There are more "wanna be divas" who play extra roles, are totally unheard of, and are not working actresses, than there are true divas in Hollywood and New York combined!

As a publicist, I am well known and well respected in the entertainment community. However, I am less experienced, I have less training, and fewer "professional" tools at my disposal, than the average publicist in Atlanta. I recently met with a producer from Aftermath records who heard about me through one of his business associates. He said, "Man, I heard that you were quiet like a lamb, but your work is ferocious like a lion". Interesting. Someone that I didn't know came from California to pay me top dollar because of what he heard. After our meeting, he paid for his work upfront, because he said that he felt he could trust me. That's business, and it's always personal.

- Troya Sampson

TASKS:

1) Become a likeable individual.... A *"people"* person.
2) Smile & laugh more.
3) Keep breath mints handy.
4) Be cordial and respectful with strangers. You never know whom an individual knows or may be.
5) Be alert in public. You never know who's watching.
6) Stay in contact with influential people, especially when you DON'T need anything from them. That way, they won't mind you contacting them when you DO need something.
7) Be humble, yet confident.

Hotep credits the leveraging of personal relationships as his main method for getting media coverage early in his career. As his influence and work grew in popularity so did his appearances in print, online, radio and TV.

hotep book signing

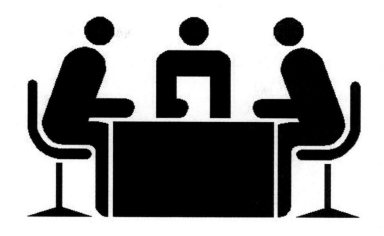

THE 7TH THING
EVERY LEADER
MUST KNOW

EVERYTHING IS NEGOTIABLE, EVERYTHING.

CHAPTER 7: EVERYTHING IS NEGOTIABLE, EVERYTHING

Successful people all have very similar characteristics. Most are very bold or brave in some way. They take chances and have confidence. One of the most prominent characteristics I've noted in successful people is an attitude that doesn't permit them to accept things at face value. They simply refuse to accept the cards that are dealt to them.

***"It's not the hand that you're dealt, but how you play with the cards!"* – Ludacris**

As a hustler in your field, one of the most powerful understandings you can have is the knowledge that, Everything is negotiable..........EVERYTHING!

Side Note:

When I say everything is negotiable, I am <u>NOT</u> including spiritual laws. God's laws cannot be negotiated. I am also <u>NOT</u> saying that you should act as if you are above the laws of your country. What I <u>AM</u> saying is: *"If a man made it, a man can change it."*

Never settle for anything that comes *standard*. When a lawyer hands you a contract, don't be afraid to negotiate. When a customer says "no", don't take that as the final answer. When a contractor/ company quotes you a price for a service, don't be afraid to talk them down. Remember...that *contract*, "*no*" and *price quote* was the *standard*, it was not designed for you. It applies to everyone else EXCEPT you; because you know that **everything is negotiable**.

LIFE LESSON:

*Recently, I needed a rental car for entertaining friends of mine. So before I went to the car rental, I decided that I was going to ask for the "preferred customer rate". (I thought I made this category up.) As soon as I walked into the car rental office, I looked for the "person in charge." As he approached, he asked if he could help me. I said plainly, "I need your preferred customer weekend rate." "Sure," he responded. I got a **mid size** car for $19.99 per day with unlimited mileage instead of the usual $39.99 per day rate. All it took was me convincing **myself** that I **deserved** the preferred customer rate. The rest was easy. Everything is negotiable. Sign the contract with **yourself** first.*
- Will Coleman, Ph.D.

LIFE LESSON:

Any astute businessperson will tell you that negotiation is an essential part of closing a deal. Even the standard terms found in contracts are negotiable in the art of business. When I did my first movie "The Sun Will Rise", I had to negotiate contracts with crew members and cast. I wanted well-known celebrities to play as my principal characters. Operating on a modest budget, financially, I could not afford their usual rates. However, I knew as social beings, we are all subjective and have changeable opinions.

I was able to negotiate more favorable terms, and the movie was made for less than one-third of the projected cost. If I had not known that everything is negotiable, I would have proved the all naysayers

right when they stated, "you don't have enough capitol to pull this thing off".
- Rahiem Shabazz

Yes, everything is negotiable. But only if two conditions are met first:

1. **You must be in a position of power to negotiate.**
2. **You must negotiate with a person in power.**

You must be in a position of power to negotiate. What are you bringing to the table? Why does the other side need to do business with you? If you haven't established a position of VALUE in the eyes of the opposing side, you may find that you have nothing to negotiate with!

You must negotiate with a person in power. All too often we get into negotiations with a front man (or woman). These people are usually the ones that will recite "the rules" and standard practices of the company to you. If you propose anything different, they will either say NO or they will have to *"check with the boss".* Skip the front man and negotiate only with the decision-maker!

"Never let someone tell you NO, that can't tell you YES." - Cocktails

TASKS:

1) **Be confident in yourself AND your offer.**
2) **Find creative ways to BARTER (exchange) services or goods as opposed to paying money for them.**
3) **When negotiating, always remember that the other party is your EQUAL, not superior.**

4) Make sure that you are negotiating with a person that actually has the *authority* to make the decision.
5) Have a lawyer look at lengthy contracts before you sign.
6) Whenever possible, request or draft contracts in "Layman's" terms instead of *Legalese*. (Legalese is simply the language lawyers use to confuse people that didn't go to law school. It allows them to charge ridiculous prices for their services.)
7) Use the term "agreement" instead of *contract*. It is less intimidating to the other party.
8) Remember that a contract is simply an agreement between two parties. It can be verbal, written or recorded on tape. It DOES NOT have to be drafted by an attorney to be enforceable. There are even stories of agreements written on <u>napkins</u> that were upheld in a court of law.

Using great negotiation skill, Hotep was able to get a movie theater to agree to screen his movie for a week. On opening night, his film, **Independent Doin' Major Things** ranked #1 at the box office; even beating **Harry Potter 4**!

THE 8TH THING
EVERY LEADER
MUST KNOW

IT'S NOT WHAT YOU KNOW <u>OR</u> WHO YOU KNOW... IT'S WHO KNOWS YOU!

CHAPTER 8: IT'S NOT *WHAT* YOU KNOW <u>OR</u> *WHO* YOU KNOW............ IT'S WHO KNOWS YOU

"Life is a game. Losers are those that don't know how to play."

We've already established that much of the game of life is won (or lost) because of relationships. Yes, business is personal, but let me take this idea a step further.

Life is one big popularity contest!

There is a popular saying that states, *"It's not **what** you know, it's **who** you know."* It's with this understanding that people commonly employ a practice known as *"name-dropping"*. Name-dropping is when a person makes a point to state that they are acquainted with certain celebrities or influential people. This is done to make the *name-dropper* appear to be important, because he/ she knows "important" people. The idea is, to *know* lots of key people in the industry so you can get preferential treatment. (*After all, business IS personal.*)

The fact is: anyone can claim to know somebody else. So, a more important question would be; **Does the celebrity or influential person that you claim to be acquainted with, KNOW YOU?** (and if they do, what do you think about you?)

It's not *what* you know, or *who* you know..... it's who knows <u>you</u>!

LIFE LESSON:

In my everyday workings, I have tried to network by doing the right thing by others. In turn, my character

speaks for itself. Many times over, I may help someone through my association with different organizations, especially with my alma mater, Morehouse College. As an assistant football coach, I travel throughout the south recruiting. Some students I recruit for football and others just to get a young man in somebody's college or university. I find my self-receiving emails, phone calls, letters, and sometimes even office visits from people that have been given my name as a reference point of contact for different opportunities. These opportunities include job offers, student-athletes wanting to transfer to Morehouse College, speaking invitations, amongst others. This is because I put myself in that position to be KNOWN verses trying to know everybody.
- Phillip Thomas

LIFE LESSON:

You can have the best product in the world, but if no one knows it, what's the point? In my city, local radio is very beneficial, especially to the small entertainment companies. However, being that Atlanta's radio market is top 10 in the nation, the cost of a radio advertisement is MAD HIGH! (Like 2 G's for a commercial high.)

My business partner, Abyss, and I had been hustling around the city, hitting every spot on the mic, and passing out our flyers for shows. It just so happened that one of the poets that is a regular on the radio came through our spot and loved the vibe. She in turn invited us to the radio station to meet the personality that put her on every week during her night slot. From that instant, the rest they say is history. We immediately hit it off. This radio

62

personality was sweet, positive, and had genuine love of our art. The poet that invited us through was a good person as well, but still worked a 9 to 5, and wasn't able to get out as often. So we offered the radio personality our street hustle and knowledge of where the hottest of the hot were, in exchange for her knowledge and support of the radio waves. It was, and still is a beautiful marriage. We started producing poetry shows for her, and had instant success. Her listeners really wanted to experience what she did on a weekly basis, but were blown away by the talent that we provided for the events. Again, we knew we had the best product, and people were going to know about it. We were the first company to sell out a 900-seat venue OFF OF POETRY! And we did it a few times. All the while, meeting and building rapports with other radio personalities in different time slots, the promotions team, all the way to the interns. We became part of their family.
- E. Christopher "Cocktails" Cornell

LIFE LESSON:

(This is as real as it gets.) I am an actor out of N.Y. One of the number one questions posed to actor is "Do you have an agent"? I have been in the game for eight years and I have worked with several agents. I like them, I love, and yes to some degree you do need them. I moved to California for a few years, and have been on some of the top T.V. stations and performed in major motion pictures. How? Based off of WHO KNEW ME; that's how. I had established myself in New York and built a rep for myself by working with some good directors, acting coaches, and other fellow actors all who had been in the business longer than myself. I informed these colleagues of my voyage to Hollywood and they did

the rest. Some passed me contact numbers and others even made phone calls on my behalf. The people who knew me, and my ability, got me through doors most people couldn't even imagine. Real Talk. This is an example of what makes this commandment so real for me in my life. Don't get it twisted... an agent is very pertinent and very much necessary, but that is a sad excuse not to get your hustle up, and do what you have to do to get your name known. Peace and God bless.

-Tyson Hall

P.S. Since I have had these experiences, I now refer to God as my agent. Who knows you better than HIM?

TASKS:

1) Revisit tasks for *"Business is Personal"*.
2) Develop a good reputation (be honest and pay back debts).
3) Make your physical appearance one that is memorable.
4) When naming your business, use a name that is unique.
5) Create a slogan that is catchy.
6) Create a corporate identity (brand) that "stands out".
7) Aggressively promote your brand through multiple formats (online,T.V., radio, flyers, t-shirts, hats, pens.... etc.)

THE 9TH THING
EVERY LEADER
MUST KNOW

IT TAKES DOUGH, TO MAKE BREAD.

CHAPTER 9: IT TAKES DOUGH, TO MAKE BREAD

Most "business–minded" people understand this one. So, I dedicate this chapter to the *artistic* people.

The day of the "starvin' artist" is dead! There is no nobility and honor in being creative and talented, yet barely able to survive. Survival mode is the lowest level of existence. Roaches "*survive*". As human beings, we should seek to LIVE. In a capitalistic world, in order to live, you need MONEY. Point blank. Get used to it. *Money, money, money, money, money!*

Side Note: The Bible states that the "love" of money is the root of all evil. I'm not saying love money, I'm saying love LIFE!

The vast majority of artists (musical, visual, film, literary) have a nasty habit of foregoing financially beneficial opportunities in pursuit of their "art".

Many quit school, refuse to get a steady job and dress/ alter their appearance in ways that force them to live in marginalized communities filled with other wannabe artists.

The rationale for these actions is often something like, *"I can't continue school or go to work because I'm trying to pursue my artistic career so I can be happy and do my thing."*

The view of school/ work as being an obstacle to artistic goals and happiness is a foolish one indeed. For many, it is just a poor excuse for being **lazy**, **irresponsible** and **broke**.

The mentality of the "starvin' artist" actually undermines the artistic freedom, creativity and integrity that they claim to seek. Once you make your survival dependent on your art, you place yourself in a position where you often have to compromise your art just to get by (this is known as artistic prostitution, or *selling out*).

EVERYBODY has some type of artistic ability; but many artists fail to recognize the difference between art and BUSINESS!

Business- *a commercial or mercantile activity engaged in as a means of livelihood.*

ARE YOU SEEKING TO TURN YOUR *ART* INTO A BUSINESS?

FACT: In the recording business, it is well known that only 10% of the albums released annually make a profit.

This success rate is similar across the board for the movie, fashion and publishing industries. (Those who go to college are referred to as *"the talented tenth".*)

FACT: Few people get paid for their art. Out of this few, only a fraction make enough money from their art to SURVIVE.

Instead of selling *art*, many artists end up *"selling-out"* because they finally have to face the fact: when turning art into business, IT TAKES *DOUGH* TO MAKE BREAD.

LIFE LESSON:

When my husband / producer / writer passed away in 2002, there was a settlement for wrongful death awarded to me. I took that money and made the biggest investment of my life....MY WORK!

Though the death of my husband is hard for me on a daily basis, I knew I must continue our work and strive for success at all times.

I decided to create a pioneer performance group called the CAUSTIC DAMES, build a company, recording studio and executive staff for CAUSTIC ENTERTAINMENT GROUP, LLC. It was the best investment I ever made!

Through in-house & internet distribution, in-house marketing, promotions & manufacturing, I have built an empire that will sustain many, many, many generations in my family for years to come, GENERATIONAL WEALTH!

Now, I run my label and production company and deposit the checks. It took the settlement money of my beloved husband's death to really cause a huge impact for my company's growth financially.

Money is the most important factor when you are starting a newbusiness. You can't start or run a real business without it.
- Mimi Johnson

R. I. P. TRUBBLE PHUNK (1964-2002) I love and miss you dearly.

LIFE LESSON:

I have been in some business or another since I was 12. Collecting bottles and old newspapers was my first business. I used to get a penny a pound for the newspapers and 2 cents per bottle for the bottles. Back in those days they actually reused the bottles.

It didn't take much money to start that business; A wagon and a pair of shoes. My dad spotted me the money for both.

Later on in life, I would become involved in various other money-making ventures. I was the son of a schoolteacher, who worked about 4 jobs to keep food on the table for the six of us. There wasn't too much family "venture capital" money left to fund any of my other ideas so I always had to figure things out on my own. My 85-year-old mom to this day does not know what I do for a living and often ask why I don't get a real job with the Telephone Company or Gas and Electric Company.

I worked many years as a commissioned salesman. It didn't take much money to get into that business beyond the cost of a few suits and a pair of shoes (my Dad had stopped buying them for me at that point) but it still cost money.

My first business that required more than a pair of shoes to get started was a game business. My buddy and I sold two local grocers on fronting the money needed to get started with that venture. The grocers were given a percentage of the new company.

My current business was started with five credit cards of $5000ea. That business has converted that $25,000 debt into a multi-million dollar publishing services company with thousands of customers.

What does all of the above have to do with you? Unless you just want to go get a job, work forty years and maybe get a pension, it takes money to make money. There are creative ways of coming up with the money but it's up to you. It also may take a couple steps to get to where you want to be. That's no big deal. If what you really want to do costs $10,000 to get started and you only have $1000, you may need to do something that only costs $1000 to get started and save from that until you have $10,000 and then go back to what you wanted to do in the first place.

A word of note: Don't burn bridges. If someone has done you a favor and extended you credit or loaned you money, pay them back.... Always. Not doing so always has a way of coming back to haunt you.
- Ron Pramschufer

TASKS:

1) **Try to finance your ventures with your own money. When you use other people's money you often subject your art / business to their opinions, guidelines and influence. YOU'RE NOT A BUSINESS OWNER IF YOU DON'T *OWN* YOUR BUSINESS!**
2) **Get a JOB, so you can afford to be a true artist/ visionary...*unbought and unbossed*!**
3) **Use your job to finance your art/ business.**
4) **Get a GOOD financial advisor.**
5) **Seek grants b4 seeking a loan.**
6) **Look for celebrities, athletes or otherwise extremely rich people to be investors in your vision. These people make great silent partners because they have so much money, and/ or are so busy they don't want to get too involved with your business. (A silent partner is basically someone who**

provides money to assist with your venture, but doesn't tell you how to run it.)

7) *STAY IN SCHOOL!* Dropping out of High School in hopes of winning a 1 in 10 gamble is crazy! College will truly be the best years of your life! It is there, that you will build your network of lifetime friends, future Fortune 500 business owners, political leaders and media moguls.

Remember: WEALTH IS NOT AN AMOUNT OF *MONEY*; IT IS A <u>STATE OF MIND</u>. THE WEALTHIEST MAN IS NOT HE WHO HAS THE *MOST*, BUT HE WHO NEEDS THE **LEAST**.

Hotep's advice to new business owners: *Keep your day job and Hustle While You Work.*

THE 10TH THING EVERY LEADER MUST KNOW

KNOW & BELIEVE IN THYSELF.

CHAPTER 10: KNOW & BELIEVE IN THYSELF

Action, self-reliance, the vision of self and the future have been the only means by which the oppressed have seen and realized the light of their own freedom.
- Marcus Garvey

In order to make the *dough*, *negotiate*, build a great *network*, develop an *image* and deal with being *lonely*; **knowledge of self is key**.

Have you ever seen an individual that appeared to be extremely lucky? Someone who success and happiness seem to follow like a shadow? Imagine reaching a point in your life where **your plans** are directly in line with that which is **planned for you**. This is the power of knowing yourself.

Everyone has a purpose on this earth, a destiny; but few actually realize what their purpose really is. Most people die having spent their entire lives searching to find the reason for their existence. Many work (and will retire from) jobs that they never enjoyed. Those that had the opportunity to try different careers, usually give up the search to *"find their place in the world"* after experiencing too many failed attempts. **To live a purpose driven life is a blessing indeed!**

From birth, each of us has been bestowed with divine gifts. We call these divine gifts, ***talents***. In general, I believe our purpose in life is to achieve self-actualization by reaching 3 goals. We can only achieve these goals by knowing ourselves.

1) **Find out what our gifts are.**
2) **Hone our skills.**
3) **Use our talents for the betterment of the world.**

The first of the 3 goals is the most difficult. How does one find their gifts? Some are lucky and find theirs early; others find theirs later in life. E*xperience* is certainly the best teacher. Our life experiences teach us about ourselves. Unfortunately, most people fail to see the **lessons** in their experiences; particularly, the "*bad*" ones.

Life is Lesson.

When people make the statement, *"Everything happens for a reason"*, they often forget that it applies to the ***bad*** things as well as the good. The game of life is comprised of a series of events. As we play, we encounter a myriad of occurrences and emotions. *Love, hate, joy, sadness, triumph* and *failure* are all necessary for us to feel. These experiences and emotions are like our **human guidance system**. They teach us our likes, dislikes, strengths and weaknesses. If we pay attention to both our positive and negative responses to life's incidents they will guide us to the realization of where our natural gifts lie.

The saddest thing in the world is wasted talent.

School is a great place to try-out, test and hone our skills. What were the things you were good at in school? Were you a great writer, mathematician, artist, speaker, athlete? **View school as an opportunity to hone your talents!** Join different clubs, teams or other extra-curricular activities. College is another stone on which you can further sharpen your sword. Take advantage of the opportunity!

The workplace can also be used to hone our talents. Whether it's a paid job or volunteer internship position, your work should be viewed as an opportunity to test your skills and further hone your talents. Try different jobs; accept new responsibilities. For each position, take note of how the job makes you feel and how well you do. Every experience is refining your skills and guiding you closer to a more intimate knowledge of yourself.

Use what you *got*, to get what you want.

Many people are overwhelmed by the game of life. They suffer continuous losses because they pursue goals that are not in-line with their natural blessings. Maybe life wouldn't be so hard if people stopped *searching* for blessings, and started *using* the ones they already have.

It is almost sinful for you to NOT utilize the gifts God has bestowed upon you.

All of our divine gifts, talents and natural skills can lead to a business that brings us sense of purpose. Best of all, our lives will be relatively *"easy"* because we would have built our welfare off of things that we enjoy and come naturally to us.

By knowing ourselves, identifying our talents and honing our skills we can make the world a better place. Each of us is unique and cannot be duplicated. The world needs us to realize our potential and contribute our gifts to the pool of life. It would be selfish of us not to reach our potential. If we don't contribute, the world and all its inhabitants will **NEVER** be able to experience what we had to offer. The choice is up to us.

Just like the superhuman characters we read about in comics, we too can use our talents (powers) for the **betterment** or **detriment** of the world. The only difference between *heroes* and *villains* is HOW they decide to use their powers. Some choose to use their talent for Good, others, for Evil.

How will you contribute to the world?

The following is an excerpt from an article I wrote for a magazine. I think it appropriately shows the power of self-knowledge.

EXCERPT:

Knowledge Of Self was a popular phrase in Hip-Hop culture during the late eighties and early nineties. It's no surprise that this era is commonly referred to as "The Golden Age" of Hip-Hop. We were shining! Not just from the rope chains, but from knowing that we are descendents of Kings and Queens, Gods and Earths.

In the mid-nineties, the "criminal culture" was allowed to invade Hip-Hop. Kings and Queens were reduced to Thugs, Pimps and Hoes. Drug use and selling became "cool". Criminals became heroes. The "G" in Kool G Rap went from standing for Genius, to meaning Gangsta. (Damn....that's deep!)

__Understand This:__ __PEOPLE ACT IN ACCORDANCE TO HOW THEY VIEW THEMSELVES.__

Today's Hip-Hop (black urban) culture lacks true knowledge of self. This void has been replaced with an IMAGE of Gangstas, Thugs, Pimps and Hoes.

So, when we "get our hustle on", instead of identifying with our royal-selves to make earth changing power moves, many of us mis-use our abilities for common street hustles that have us constantly on the run from po-po. This is what is known as "The Trap."

The life of one of the world's greatest hustlers, Malcom X, is the perfect example of how Knowledge Of Self can transform ones life. Peep how his hustle abilities went from "street corner" to "earth mover" once he learned who he truly was.

If you really want to step your game up, instead of wasting money on weed, and alcohol.........buy a book. Instead of the strip club, visit a museum. Watch the history channel, instead of Scarface (for the 30th time). Instead of freestyle ciphers, participate in a knowledge-building cipher. Real hustlers and gangstas make matter move, BUT also make moves that matter. Ask Carter "G" Woodson. (AUC Magazine Feb 2006)

Believing in yourself is easy. Once you have gained knowledge of self you will have also realized that God has been with you every step of your life's journey. In fact, you would have learned that God was not only **with** you, he was **WITH-IN** you as well. What better reason to believe in yourself is there?

TASKS:

1) **Take a personality test.**
2) **Meditate.**
3) **Recognize that God is *within you*, as much as he is all around you.**
4) **Study your history/ culture.**
5) **Video yourself so you can see yourself the way others see you.**
6) **Study human psychology.**
7) **Self- analyze.**

8) Go to a college outside of your hometown.
9) Ask people their opinion of you.
10) Ask people their first impression of you.
11) Read other self-empowerment books.
12) Identify & *Utilize* your strengths.
13) Identify & *Improve* on your weaknesses.
14) Read this book again!

Most people don't know that the name "Hotep" is Egyptian/ African. It means **PEACE**. Hotep (pictured here visiting The Valley of The Kings in Egypt) is named after **Imhotep**, who is known to be the world's first multi-genius, scientist, mathematician and builder of the first pyramid.

THE FINAL ANALYSIS:

The moral of the story is: *Life is what YOU make it!*

YOU are in control!
YOU are responsible!
YOU are at fault!
YOU can change it!

If you can imagine life being a popular video game; YOU are the one that holds the controller. The more you *"play"*, the better your skills get. You learn how to navigate more easily. Your use of time becomes more efficient. If you *"lose"*, you hit the **continue** button and press on. You keep going because that is the ONLY way you can eventually **win**.

Following this analogy, I hope you use **10 Things Every Leader Must Know** like a manual for this intense video game called *Life*. It is a reference guide that provides easy answers to difficult questions. Refer to it as often as necessary for "*insider tips*". Not to be confused for short-cuts, the principals herein give you a better understanding of the dynamics of the game, which in turn, will ultimately make you a better *player*.

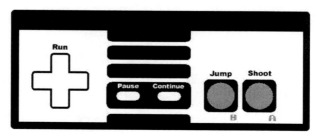

Peace & Power!

- Hotep

A NOTE TO PARENTS & EDUCATORS:

Over the course of my 14-year teaching career, I've noticed that our public educational system fails our youth miserably. Not because it is inferior, but because of how we teach our youth to use it. We basically tell children that they should **get an education, so they can be smart, so they can pursue a degree, that will land them a good job, and make them a lot of money, so they can be happy.**

Well, besides wrongfully equating money with happiness, we as a society also make the mistake of **lying** to our youth.

We live in a country where high school dropouts become millionaires, and college graduates struggle living check to check. In our great nation, a person can make more money throwing a ball, than ones who save lives, educate our future and protect our civil liberties..... **combined!**

The high school dropout rate in some areas is up to **50%** because our youth know the old model of *"go to school to get a good job"* is dead. **Why should they bother going to school?**

The TRUTH shall set you free!

10 Things Every Leader Must Know is based off of true, real-life success stories, business best practices, ancient wisdom and simple common sense. The practice of these ideals compels the reader to seek greatness; ALL READERS, yes, **even our hardheaded youth!**

Instead of viewing school as an *obstacle*, they will begin to see it as an **opportunity!** They will see their teachers as **allies**, as opposed to *enemies*. They will understand that **it's lonely at the top**, and therefore, won't be afraid to excel when most fail. Peer pressure will be less of a problem. They will know that their **network is their net worth**, so they will choose their friends more wisely. They will want to dress more appropriately, because they learned that **image is everything**. They will show up to class early because they understand how **the early bird gets the worm**. They will take a renewed interest in history and science, so they can **know their self**. They will actually seek to improve their writing, reading and speaking skills because they now see the TRUE connection between school, the real world and their own lives as future moguls, inventors, educators, entrepreneurs and, (of course) leaders,!

"The ULTIMATE HUSTLER is one who is both book smart and street smart. He/she is able to take a good education, combine it with common sense, to make dollars and cents!"

–Hotep, President of Hustle University.org

Hotep uses *10 Things Every Leader Must Know* to teach leadership and encourage achievement in Middle and High Schools as well.

BREAKDANCE
Copyright 2003

The strobe light's in full effect tonight,
my gold rope's glistening……. it reflect the light.
Expect the wife to be upset,
it's only right that a brother go out and do his thing no
regrets.
The local radio station's havin' Old School Night,
I'm almost 30,
and fit the category.
My life's now surrounded by move- fakers,
it felt good to see brothers when they broke out the
windbreakers.
I was the type,
on the opposite side,
scoping the hype,
got a brother open tonight,
like sitting front row at an Ali fight,
or the first time you ever heard Rapper's Delight.
We was just teens,
Mantronix hit the scene,
honey dips in their Bengal earrings,
always caught my eye,
under fresh Cazelles,
that I boosted from 42nd and Canal.

I represent grown folks and showboats,
bicycles, we put the cards in our own spokes.
I take a fat black marker and write love,
for anyone who ever wore a shiny white glove,
and spun, on linoleum,
the Royal Crown Petroleum,
to make waves…..
stocking caps with a hole in them.
No doubt,
it was better than armor,
in the 6th Grade with a new black leather bomber.

In fact, I always wanted a sheepskin,
but moms was cheap then,
I never got more than a hat.
Striped Lee's and shell toes,
musta' been the fact that hell froze,
who ever thought that it would come back.

In '89 hot shot in Nintendo,
used to have crazy dreams: fancy cars and limos.
Hip-Hop creshendo,
write with a broken pencil,
now they all call me Mr. Benzo.
Doin' a show up in SoHo,
bums on the street tryin' ta get my dough....
I said "No".
Used to rock beats on promos,
now we shake hands with the lames and momos.
I know it's sick.
Stop dis-ease,
brother's used to rock for free,
now we play Monopoly.
And we cop with ease,
all properties,
and material items for girls that's knock knee'd.
I go for broke.
Look at the state of the world,
I show them hope,
travel upstream....... in a rowboat.
Player, I got more bars than soap.
Forever holding it down,
my vision is long scope.

-Hotep

ABOUT THE AUTHOR:

Hotep is president and founder of HustleUniversity.Org, the first self-help HBCU for entrepreneurs. He is an internationally renowned success strategist, Congressional Award-winning educator and entrepreneur known for his out-the-box thinking, guerilla marketing tactics, branding expertise and his unique "no nonsense"  approach to teaching leadership, entrepreneurship and practical business best practices.

Hotep's work has earned him nominations as a CNN Hero and for the U.S Presidential Citizen's Award. Hotep calls himself a "Business Abolitionist" and considers entrepreneurship as the key to freedom for all people. He is also the author of several popular empowerment books including the phenomenal classic; The Hustler's 10 Commandments.

Hotep says, *"With the right mentality there is nothing that can STOP you; with the wrong mentality, nothing can SAVE you!"*

To Book Hotep for Speaking Contact:
404-294-7165
hustleuinc@gmail.com
www.HustleUniversity.Org

CONTRIBUTING WRITERS:

Nancy Gilliam is an accomplished performing artist, author and teacher. Her media credits include working with the MGM and ABC Television.Her author credits include: the companion study guide to the biography for Lebron James, "Chicken Soup for the African American Soul" and "Chicken Soup for the African American Woman's Soul".A true believer in empowerment and education, she is the co-founder of the African American Literary & Media Group.

Will Coleman, Ph.D. is Co-Founder and Co-Director of the Black Kabbalah Institute. It is a nonsectarian organization that is designed to teach and apply principles of the Hebrew mysticism for the enrichment of African/Americas spiritual and psychological health. He is an ordained minister and Theologian-in-Residence at First Afrikan Church in Lithonia, Georgia.

Allen Johnston created THE MUSIC SPECIALIST website (www.asha.com); a website dedicated to education of the entertainment industry. His latest book "Publishing Quick & Easy" is a mainstay for new and experienced attorneys. Currently, Mr. Johnston develops International & National movie, audio and publishing deals for major and independent artists and film makers.

Queen is an internationally known spoken word artist from South Jersey. Queen has appeared on many national television networks, such as, BET's 106 and Park, NBC, UPN and the likes. With two published books, and two albums, she is now writing and producing movies. Queen has toured the US several times. To find out more about Queen, visit www.Justqueen.net.

Mr. Shabazz is a recognized hip-hop journalist with credentials in writing video treatments, movie scripts, bios, press releases, magazine articles, and online articles. As owner of RASHA ENTERTAINMENT LLC, Rahiem produced the feature film, "The Sun Will Rise". He is in the process of negotiating for the picture's worldwide distribution. Currently, he is working on his first novel titled "Love On Lay-Away".

Omar Tyree, a New York Times best-selling author and 2001 NAACP Image Award recipient for Outstanding Literature in Fiction, has sold more than 1.4 million copies of books worldwide. Most recently, Tyree began Flyy Girl Incorporated, based on his most successful novel and beautiful career women of color. He also plans to launch a book-related television program to reinforce the seriousness of African-American literature. For more on Omar Tyree, goto (*www.OmarTyree.com*)

Tyson is a native New Yorker; his roots run deep into the pulse of the NY cultural/theater scene. His love for fashion/music/dance drew him to the stage as a model and dancer. After Graduating John Jay College, Tyson threw himself into developing his newly found talents in Drama. His professionalism has elevated his worth and given him work with respected directors and films, such as, **"PAID IN FULL"** and television roles on **New York Undercover**, **Moesha** and **OZ**.

Ron Pramschufer is one of the founders of RJ Communications and Booksjustbooks.com. He co-invented and marketed two highly successful satirical political board games. The idea of RJ Communications and Booksjustbooks.com evolved from a combination of past experiences in the production office of a book manufacturer, in a pressroom bindery-shipping department and as a partner in a small press publisher. *Contact Ron at ron@rjcom.com*.

Phillip Thomas is an assistant football coach at his alma mater, Morehouse College. He is active in community service ventures through non-profit organizations where he sits as a board member of 99ways Youth Foundation and The Project Friendship Foundation. Phil is also completing course work for obtaining his doctorate degree in Educational Leadership. Phil resides in Ellenwood, Georgia.

Troya Sampson is an actress, publicist and former educator. She has landed roles in feature films such as *The Gospel*, *Madea's Family Reunion*, and *ATL*, as well as other independent films and shorts. In addition to pursuing acting, Troya is working independently as a publicist for various artists in the entertainment industry. One of Troya's favorite quotes of is, "success is a journey, not a destination".

Mimi Johnson has operated Caustic Entertainment Group, LLC, since the death of her husband in 2002 alone. She is responsible for all of the bookings, executive production, copyrights/ publishing of their work, manufacturing and distribution of their product which includes current CD, "ESTROGEN LOVE LP". Go to www.causticdames.com for more info.

Tarik Scott aka Big Tah, CEO of BTM, National Director of Dynamic Producer, Co CEO of World Premiere and Co Manager of Willie Joe. Big Tah has a BA in Music Industry Studies/Marketing. He is a self-professed Marketing Genius and applies it to many hats such as event planning, artist management, consultation and promotions.

E. Christopher "Cocktails" Cornell is author of Cocktails Commentary: Volume 1 and the founder of Live Poets Society, L.L.C with his business partner, HBO Def Poet, Derrick "Abyss" Graham. Along with producing quality spoken word events, the company offers a multi-faceted approach to events planning. Cocktails has appeared on MTV Road Rules 11 and is one of the feature entertainers on Joyce Littel's Love and Relationship Cruise for V-103. Visit **www.livepoets.net** for more info.

Keisha Perry is an Entertainment Attorney licensed to practice in Georgia. Ms. Perry worked as a Business Law Consultant for Better Communications, Inc. where she was primarily responsible for entity formations for small business owners. Since establishing The Perry Law Group, Ms. Perry has led entity formations for independent labels, drafted and negotiated contracts for artists, producers, and songwriters. Ms. Perry has the tenacity, knowledge, and perseverance that it takes to be successful and build long-term and prosperous working relationships.

Lead by example first!

- Hotep

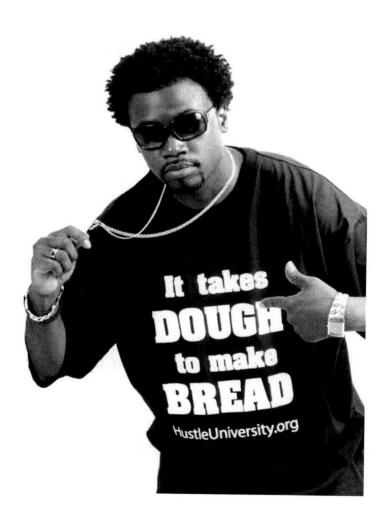

OTHER PROGRAMS:

Poster, Lesson Guide/ Intervention Kit & Textbook

Lesson Guide/ Intervention Kit & Textbook

Lesson Guide & Textbook

CURRICULUM AVAILABLE: